GAZING

Encountering the Mystery of Art

Stephen R. Turley, Ph.D.

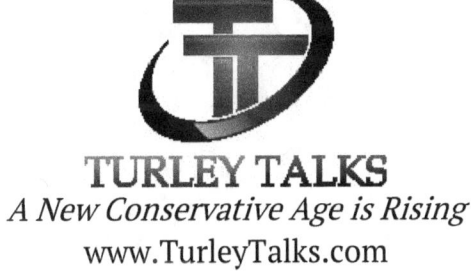

TURLEY TALKS
A New Conservative Age is Rising
www.TurleyTalks.com

Copyright © 2018 by Dr. Steve Turley. All Rights Reserved.

ISBN-13: 978-1719589772

ISBN-10: 1719589771

No part of this publication may be reproduced, stored in a retrieval system, or transmitted in any form or by any means, electronic, mechanical, photocopying, recording, scanning, or otherwise, except as permitted under Section 107 or 108 of the 1967 United States Copyright Act, without either the prior written permission of the author, or authorization through payment of the appropriate per-copy fee to the Copyright Clearance Center, Inc., 222 Rosewood Drive, Danvers, MA 01023, (978) 750-8400, or on the web at www.copyright.com. Requests to the author for permission should be addressed to steve@turleytalks.com.

Table of Contents

Preface   7

Introduction: A Theology of Art and Sight   9

Chapter 1: Andrei Rublev, *The Holy Trinity* (c. 1410-1425)   15

Chapter 2: Leonardo Da Vinci, *The Last Supper* (1495-1498)   23

Chapter 3: Michelangelo, *Pietà* (1498-1500)   31

Chapter 4: Raphael, *School of Athens* (1509-1511)   39

Chapter 5: Caravaggio, *The Beheading of Saint John the Baptist* (1608)   47

Chapter 6: Rembrandt, *The Prodigal Son* (1663-1669)   55

Chapter 7: Gabriel Rossetti, *Ecce Ancilla Domini* (1850)   61

Chapter 8: Vincent van Gogh, *The Starry Night* (1889)   67

About Turley Talks   76

About the Author   78

PREFACE

If I've heard it once, I've heard it a thousand times: "How on earth do I teach my students to love and appreciate good art"? "It's embarrassing, but the fact is I really don't know how to appreciate a good painting myself"! "My students just don't seem to buy why certain masterpieces are any better than the latest anime or manga"!

I've even heard variations on this theme. Math teachers have asked me: "How can I show my students the beauty of math? I'd love to use art and famous paintings, but I'm not sure how." Administrators have complained: "We want the walls of our school to be beautiful; unfortunately, many of us don't know how to show our students why these great works of art are ... well ... great." And I hear it every year from a new crop of young students at both the high school and college level: "Isn't art just a matter of opinion? Who are you to say which art is good or bad for the rest of us"?

If you're struggling with these issues, this book was written specifically for you. Whether you're an art teacher, or humanities teacher, a math or science teacher, an administrator, or homeschooling parent, this book will equip you to be able to enrich your classes and teaching with multiple encounters with great art. In the pages that follow, you will be introduced to some of the greatest works of art ever created. For each piece, you will get

- A brief bio of the artist
- An explanation of the artwork
- Sample questions with answers to help facilitate classroom discussions

In addition, you will learn:

- How to understand and explain a theology of art
- How to practice gazing and learn to sanctify the soul and sight
- How to introduce great works of art into your classroom lesson plans
- How to lead your students to contemplate works of art

There's no longer any reason to be intimidated or frustrated with teaching students to love and appreciate artistic masterpieces. With this book, you will experience the thrill of awakening students to the limitless wonder of pictorial beauty, and in so doing, deepen and enrich your own appreciation and vision, as together you encounter the mystery of art.

INTRODUCTION

A Theology of Art and Sight

Throughout my life, there have been two books that have shaped my understanding and appreciation of great art. The first was given to me by my childhood babysitter, Mary Apuzzo, an elderly Italian woman who helped to raise my sister and me as both our parents pursued their careers in chemistry. After a sojourn to her ancestral homeland, she brought back a book for me simply entitled *Michelangelo.* It was an English edition of the life and work of one of the greatest artists of all time. She knew I loved to draw and paint, and she was my most devoted patron, sustaining my artistry with her endless adoration and gracious encouragement. I adored that book. Through it, I became immersed in the sculptures, paintings, and architecture of this Tuscan genius. Even now, as I write, the book sits in front of me, inviting me, as it has all these years, to encounter its pages of endless beauty.

The second book that shaped by artistic sensibilities came to me in the darkest moment of my life. In August of 1980, my father died suddenly, leaving behind a heartbroken and grieving family. He was only 47 years old. In the day or two leading to the funeral, my paternal grandfather handed me a book, *Rembrandt's Life of Christ.* He told me that, once upon a time, my father noticed it on my grandfather's bookshelf, and remarked that he thought I would very much appreciate its contents. My grandfather handed the book to me as a token of his love and as a perpetual reminder of the gift of beauty that was my father.

These two books would be inordinately influential in shaping my theology of art and sight.

A Theology of Art: Christ and Creation

In his work, *Voicing Creation's Praise: Towards a Theology of the Arts*, Jeremy Begbie roots a distinctively Christian vision of art in the colossal significance of the humanity of Christ for the remaking of the cosmos.[1] Following the witness of the New Testament, Begbie notes that the entire cosmos has been incorporated into the transformative life, death, and resurrection of Christ, such that in Christ, the new creation has already begun:

> The resurrection of the crucified humanity of Christ is itself the embryonic promise for the entire physical cosmos. *In him* all things have already been made new, and *in him* the destiny of creation has been set forth. Thus, to speak of Christ as the 'end' of creation (in the manner of e.g. Rev. 3:14) is not merely to speak of his supremacy or of his decisiveness in bring creation to completion, it is also to say that in his very Person, as the risen and ascended God-Man, he embodies and constitutes the *telos* of created reality.[2]

---

[1] Jeremy Begbie, *Voicing Creation's Praise: Towards a Theology of the Arts* (London: T&T Clark, 1991), 175.
[2] Begbie, *Voicing,* 176, emphasis mine.

Begbie makes the sustained argument that as the darkness and death of this world is now being penetrated and overwhelmed by the light and life of Christ, a Christian theology of art celebrates our participation in this cosmic redemption by giving voice to the restoration of the created order as the future beatific vision of the redeemed cosmos has already begun to manifest itself in Christ. Through the artist's work, the future of the cosmos comes forward into time and is realized in the present, such that in and through art the final goal of history actually becomes a present reality.

A Theology of Sight: Gazing

A theology of art draws us into the notion of a theology of sight. In the Greek world, Plato considered sight the most important sense; it was appropriated as the foundation of philosophy and the sense that leads to a discovery of divine truth. In his pursuit of beauty in the *Symposium*, Plato appropriates *visual* beauty as that which initially inspires the philosopher to mount the 'heavenly ladder' to God, who is absolute beauty.

In early Christianity, visual symbolism took on significance at least in part due to the multi-ethnic nature of the growing church, in that this multi-ethnicity encouraged the use of easily recognized symbols that transcended language barriers.[3] An emerging iconography in the East sought to sanctify the visual, shaping the optical sense with earthly materials transformed into heavenly visions of new creation. It was within the Byzantine world that a cosmology of icons

---

[3] Patrick Reyntiens, "Art, Visual," in Adrian Hastings, et al, (eds.), *The Oxford Companion to Christian Thought* (New York: Oxford University Press, 2000), 41.

was forged, such that world transfigured into images of heaven revealed through the earthly life of Christ. Moreover, it was thought that through iconography our creative artistic endeavors could be incorporated into, and thereby transformed in, the transfiguring life of Christ.

Crossing over into the medieval West, the developing Augustinian theology ascribed a primacy to the sense of sight in relation to the doctrine of divine illumination. The thirteenth-century bishop Robert Grossetest (cf. 1245) wrote: "Light is truly the principle of all beauty; light, as the principle of color, is the beauty and ornament of all that is visible." Most notably developed by Bonaventure in his *Reduction of the Arts to Theology*, light became the key motif for understanding, so that just as the physical sight was dependent on physical light, so spiritual sight was dependent on a divine luminosity. Hence for Bonaventure, the illumination of the Holy Spirit upon the mind enables us to imaginatively reinterpret the natural world around us as a theatre of divine glory, a reinterpretation made explicit in the idealized work of the artisan. Divine illumination entails the overlapping of the natural world with a sanctified imagination thus transforming the world around us into visions of new creation.

This emphasis on visions of new creation required new ways of seeing, which we are calling here *gazing.* I borrow this term from Peter Pearson's work on iconography.[4] Pearson notes that we tend to see things with a rather cursory glance, in that we look at objects with the goal of sorting, defining, and

---

[4] Peter Pearson, *A Brush with God: An Icon Workbook* (Harrisburg, PA: Morehouse Publishing, 2005).

organizing them in our technology-influenced imaginations. Instead, art requires a different kind of "looking," what Pearson calls *gazing*. Art involves giving yourself entirely over to the visual experience, looking deeply into the image. The visual arts provide the opportunity to sanctify sight by uniting our eyes with our intellect, such that the depiction of divine images is experienced by both sight and soul.

The Gift of Vision

A theology of art and sight combine to awaken what classical and Christian philosophers called *theoria,* derived from a verb meaning 'to see' or 'to look.' Theoria enabled the observer to probe the world so as to see the divine meaning and purpose in all things, the eternal reality in which all things cohered. As Andrew Louth has noted, the Latin word used to translate theoria, *contemplatio*, originally meant something akin to 'what goes on in a temple,' "referring to the act of beholding the statue of the divinity enshrined in the temple."[5] This divine notion is similar to Aristotle's understanding of *intellectus* in Book 10 of his *Nichomachean Ethics*, which involved understanding the world comparable to the gods.[6]

This is why this book is subtitled *Encountering the Mystery of Art*. Because theoria awakens us to the eternal dimension reflected in the world, the classical mind recognized that true wisdom is beyond the grasp of the finite creature, man, and is indeed the possession of the gods.[7] Knowledge in its traditional sense begins in wonder and in fact ends in wonder,

---

[5] Andrew Louth, "Theology, Contemplation and the University," *Studies in Christian Ethics* (2004): 73.

[6] Louth, "Theology," 72.

[7] Andrew Louth, *Discerning the Mystery: An Essay on the Nature of Theology* (Oxford: Clarendon Press, 1983), 144.

since one is penetrating more deeply into the mystery of reality. Great art is great precisely because it awakens us to this mystery, this eternal dimension inherent in the created order, and thereby awakens a comparable wonder and awe within us.

The important dimension of gazing is *transformation*; through the practice of gazing, the artwork should transform before our very eyes. We should begin to see things that were always there but that escape the cursory glance. And in seeing the artwork transform, *we transfigure with it*! Gazing involves both the transformation of the artwork and the transformation of the observer.

***

These many years later, I often go back to those two books that acquainted me at such an early age with the divine life revealed through great art, gazing at their pictorial splendor and formative beauty. Particularly as I stare through the brush strokes represented by the Rembrandt prints, I've come to see that his depictions of the *Life of Christ* collectively constitute not simply the life Christ lived and lives, but indeed, the life he *gives,* the gift of unending life that he has procured for all that are in him. This is the life of Christ that my father – through the hands of my grandfather – ultimately shared with me.

Michelangelo and Rembrandt are among the several artists represented in the pages that follow. It is my hope that my life-changing experiences with the mystery of these masterpieces may awaken the blessing of a comparable encounter for you and your students.

CHAPTER 1

Andrei Rublev, *The Holy Trinity* (c. 1410-1425)

Bio:

Andrei Rublev (c.1360-1430) is considered the greatest medieval Russian painter. However, there is very little extant information on Rublev's life. He may have been born in Pskov, and the first mention of him is in 1405, when he painted the icons for the Cathedral of the Annunciation in Moscow. He became a monk in the Andronikov Monastery, where he spent the rest of his life. In fact, Rublev appears never to have left Moscow upon entering the monastic order. He died at the monastery in 1430.

Rublev's work is representative of a flourishing revival of Russian art after its ruin during the iconoclastic rule of the Ottomans in the Byzantine empire. Russian art was highly influenced by the iconic traditions of Byzantium, but Rublev is credited to have developed the tradition in terms of combining unprecedented artistic sophistication with ancient asceticism and piety. A synod in 1551 recognized Rublev's works as a standard for subsequent iconographers to emulate.

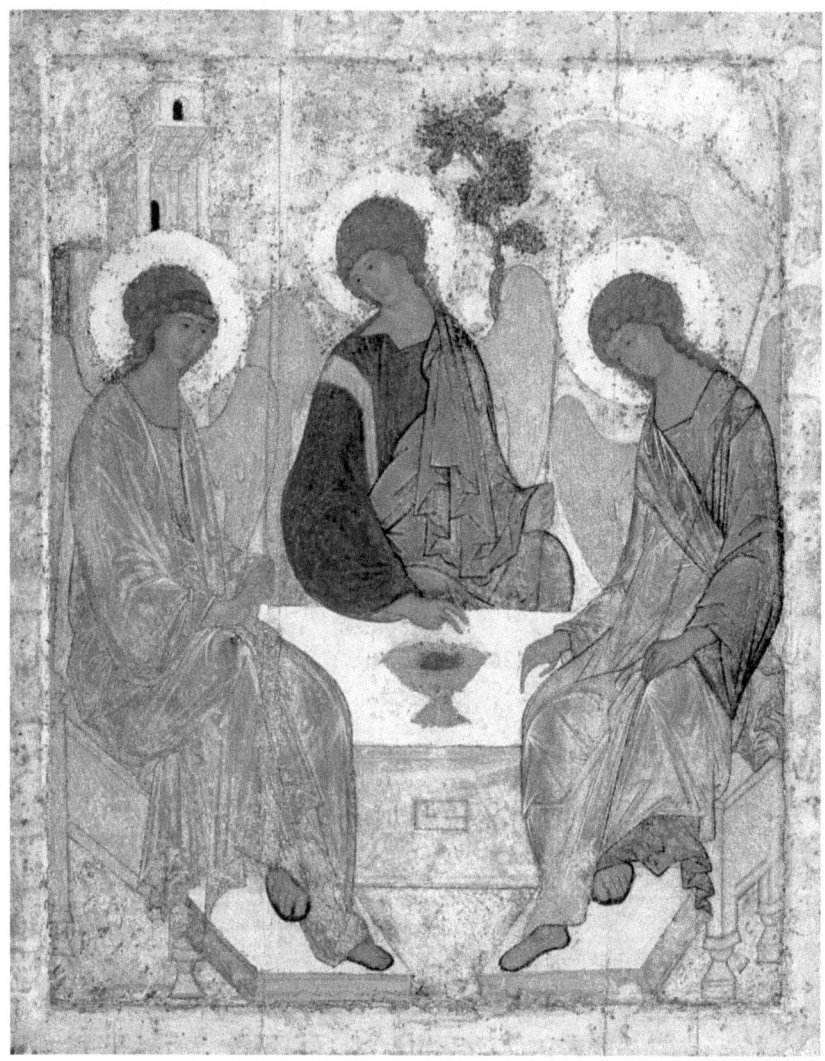

In 1988, Rublev became the first Russian painter to be canonized as a saint by the Russian Orthodox Church.

The painting:

Andrei Rublev's *Holy Trinity* is one of the finest Russian paintings in existence. He painted (technically icons are 'written'; hence the term *iconography*) the icon sometime between 1410 and 1425. It was created for Trinity Cathedral and depicts the Old Testament narrative of what is called the *Hospitality of Abraham* popularized in early Christian catacomb paintings. In Genesis 18, three angels visit Abraham and he serves them food and drink. One of them tells Sarah that she will have a son in her old age. Rublev has removed Abraham and Sarah from the scene, focusing instead in the visual revelation of the Trinity in the angelic visit. The icon is now in the Tretyakov Gallery in Moscow.

Optional Discussion Prompt:

How would you represent communion in a drawing or painting?

Give the students about 10 minutes to write down their observations while gazing at the painting.

Analysis:

What do you notice about the icon? What strikes you as interesting?

The three angels sit around a rectangular table, with a cup at the center. In the background, there's a three-level building behind the first angel on the left, a tree behind the center angel, and a mountain behind the third on the right. The angels themselves resemble one another and yet have distinctive characteristics. They share the same face, hair, halos, wings, and clothing items. But they also exemplify significant differences. The angel on the left nods towards and looks out toward the other two, while the angels in the center and right lower their heads towards the angel on the left. The angel on the left is clothed in translucent garments, while the clothing of the center and right angel is characterized by more dense and definite color patterns.

Whom do you think each angel represents?

The specific identity of each angel has been argued about for centuries. Nevertheless, there are features that do appear to identify each with some certainty. The angel on the left is generally identified with the mystery of God the Father, with one hand over the other. This is because of the translucent clothing (signifying the mystery of the Father) and the head bowing of the other two angels towards him (signifying the Father as representative of the Trinity in its absolute subsistence).

The Father gestures toward the center angel, who reciprocates with his own hand extending two fingers, signifying the two natures (divine and human) of the Incarnation. Moreover, the central angel is clothed with two garments, an inner red or crimson garment, and an outer blue garment. In the iconic tradition, Christ is depicted with these two-color schemes: red on the inside (signifying the love of God) and blue on the outside (signifying his eternity). The second angel is thus interpreted as the Son.

The Son extends his fingers towards the angel on the right, who directs the gesture downwards towards the table as the Holy Spirit. Note how his right hand seems to form the outline of a dove. The colors of his clothing would corroborate this, in that green is the color of Pentecost in the Greek East.

Thus, from left to right, we see the Father, the Son, and the Holy Spirit.

What do you make of the imagery behind the angels?

Each of the background objects goes through its own transfiguration when reinterpreted as backdrops of their respective angelic forefronts. The house behind the Father transfigures into a Temple and indeed a symbol of the New Jerusalem, the City of God, built by the Father. The tree behind the Son transfigures into the Tree of Life, which is restored to the world in the cross. And the mountain behind the Holy Spirit bends in reverence to the Trinity, perhaps as a baptismal wave, and transforms into the Holy Mountain of the Messianic Banquet of Isaiah 25.

What shapes or geometric features do you see represented in the icon?

The magnificence of the icon comes out with Rublev's use of shapes. The two dominant geometric features are the triangle and the circle. If we see the center angel's halo as the vertex, the observer's eyes move downward and sideways to the left and right corners of the table, thus revealing the triangular symbol of the Trinity. Moreover, the curvature of the halos leads the eyes to continue to draw a visual circle around the shoulders and seated positions of the right and left angels, circumscribing the symbol of eternity and unity. The Trinity is thus imagined geometrically as both one in Being and three in Person.

But then we notice that the table around which the angels sit is a rectangle, the four corners on the side and top signifying the 'four corners of the world.' Four is a cosmic number in the ancient world, signified by the four elements of the cosmos (earth, air, fire, water), the four directions (north, south, east, west), the four seasons, the four humours of the human body, etc. The mini rectangle at the front side of the table may signify the place where relics are placed within an Orthodox altar, and thus would symbolize the realm of the dead. The entire cosmos is thus enveloped by the three persons of the Trinity. As such, the Spirit's hand gesture forming the wings of a dove would evoke the creation narrative when the Spirit brooded over the primordial waters (Genesis 1:2), echoed in the recreation of the world with Noah in Genesis 8 and the baptism of Christ in Matthew 3.

What's at the center of the table, in the bowl or chalice?

It appears to be a lamb, representative of the calf that Abraham offered to them in Genesis 18, as well as the lamb of God who takes away the sins of the world (John 1:29).

What is each angel holding?

These are their walking staves, representing their royal scepters, as well as evoking the three trees of Isaiah 60:13: the cypress, cedar, and pine associated with the cross of Christ in Orthodox tradition.

But there seems to be something even more going on here. Notice the shape formed inside the fellowship of the Trinity as they gather around the table; what is that shape?

If we look to the right, beginning with the right leg of the angel on the right and follow upwards the curvature of his knee, moving our eyes wider to the right up to his right shoulder, and do the same beginning with the left leg of the left angel moving our eyes along the curvature of his knee and outward along his thigh and up towards his shoulder, we will see the right and left outline of a chalice, a magnification of the communion cup at the center. Thus, the Trinity transfigures into the symbol of infinite and eternal communion in love and delight.

What does that communion chalice mean for us?

This is perhaps the most beautiful part of the icon. The four corners of the cosmic-table are occupied by *three* figures: the Father on the left side, the Son on the backside, and the Holy Spirit on the right. Who then is to occupy the frontside? This is where the beauty of gazing reaches its climax: the frontside of the cosmic communion-table is reserved for the one who gazes at the icon. The Rublev icon is thus a beautiful icon of *invitation,* calling us to come and participate in the infinite communion of the Father, the Son, and the Holy Spirit.

CHAPTER 2

Leonardo da Vinci, *The Last Supper* (1495-1498)

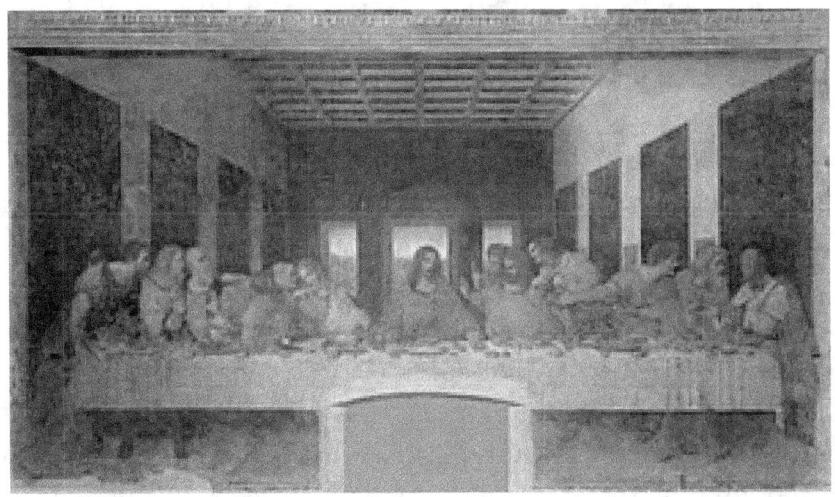

Bio:

Leonardo was born on April 15, 1452 in Vinci, part of the territory of Florence. Little is known about his early life.[8] In 1466, Leonardo became an apprentice to one of the most renowned artists and teachers of his day, Andrea di Cione,

---

[8] https://www.leonardoda-vinci.org/biography.html.

also known as Verrochio. It was here that Leonardo began to develop his artistic technique, consisting of drawing, painting, and sculpting. At twenty-years old, he was received as a master in the Guild of St. Luke, which was comprised of artists and medical doctors, and began receiving commissions to paint for various venues. These commissions brought him to Milan, where he worked from 1482 to 1499, when he fled Milan for Venice due to invading French troops during the Second Italian War. A polymath, Leonardo served as an architect and engineer, devising means to defend the city from naval attack. He returned to Florence in 1500, and continued painting as well as serving as a military architect and engineer. Shortly after returning to Milan, François I of France captured Milan, resulting in Leonardo's move to a manor house near François' residence at the royal Chateau Amboise as the king's artist. He died a few years later in France and was buried in the Chapel of Saint-Hubert in the castle of Amboise.[9]

Leonardo is universally heralded as a master of the High Renaissance (1490-1530). His skill in science and mathematics are evident in his painting skills that feature extraordinary depth and dimensionality. He's particularly noted for creating three-dimensional effects through using diagonal lines that intersect with the painting's background, particularly evident in *The Last Supper*.[10]

The painting:

Painted between 1495-98, Leonardo's *Last Supper* is considered not only a masterpiece of the High Renaissance,

---

[9] https://www.leonardoda-vinci.org/biography.html.
[10] http://www.davincilife.com/paintings.html.

but indeed one of the greatest paintings of all time. It is a mural painting that spans 15 feet x 29 feet on the wall of the refectory of the convent of Santa Maria delle Grazie in Milan. It was unfortunately painted in such a way that it began deteriorating merely decades after it was completed. Fortunately, Leonardo's students had made detailed notes of the painting, which have greatly helped in recent restoration campaigns.

The drama of the painting surrounds what Christ has just said: "Verily I say unto you: one of you will betray me." (John 13:21; Matthew 26:21) The reaction of each one of the disciples is depicted vividly by Leonardo. Arranged in four groups of three, the *Notebooks of Leonardo Da Vinci* identify the disciples from left to right as: Bartholomew, James the Less and Andrew (Group 1); Judas Iscariot, Peter, and John (Group 2); Thomas, James, and Philip (Group 3); and Jude Thaddeus, Matthew, and Simon the Zealot (Group 4). As the gospels describe the disciples questioning of whom is Jesus referring (cf. Matthew 26:22), of interest is the way Leonardo depicts Philip gesturing: "Lord, is it I"? Peter is drawn holding a knife, foreshadowing his severing of the ear of the soldier in the Garden of Gethsemane (John 18:10), and he's motioning to the one sitting next to Jesus to ask him to identify the betrayer (John 13:24).

Optional Discussion Prompt:

Why do you think this is one of the most famous paintings in the world? What makes it so appreciated?

Give the students about 10 minutes to write down their observations while gazing at the painting.

Analysis:

What do you find interesting or unusual about this painting?

The entire painting centers on Christ; indeed, his head is the point perspective for the entire picture. The figure of Christ is framed "by the central window at the back, the curved pediment of which arches above his head. The pediment is the only curve in the architectural framework, and it serves here as a halo."[11] He is clothed in his iconic colors of a blue cloak wrapped around a red garment.

How does Leonardo depict Judas?

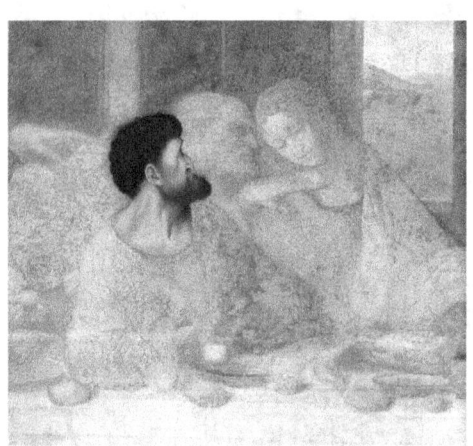

Leonardo depicts Judas in Group 2 as the betrayer: he's noticeably depicted in a shadowy form, clasping a bag of silver with his right hand, looking at Jesus, his head lower than the other disciples. His left hand (a symbol of betrayal) is reaching for the same dish as Christ's right hand, depicting Christ's words: "The one who has dipped his hand into the bowl with me will betray me." (Matthew 26:23)

How is the spaced ordered mathematically? Do you see any dominant numbers or shapes?

---

[11] Richard G. Tansey, et al, *Gardener's Art through the Ages,* Tenth Edition (Fort Worth: Harcourt Brace College Publishers, 1996), 733.

The space is ordered mathematically by threes (the Trinity) and fours (the cosmos). There are three windows behind Christ, and the apostles are all arranged in groups of three, Christ's head and outstretched arms form a triangle, and the space between him and John form an upside-down triangle. The groups of disciples are arranged in four, signifying the four gospels, which are complemented by the four tapestries on each side of the room. The eight tapestries signify the Eighth Day, the Day of Redemption, when God restores the world he created in six days and blessed on the seventh. It thus appears fitting that the tapestries on either side of the room are bridged together by the landscape in the background appearing through the three windows. Leonardo has brilliantly arranged symbols of heaven and earth together as both are embodied in Christ, being fully God and fully man.

How does Leonardo's depiction of Christ contrast with that of the disciples?

The contrast between the serene quietude of Christ and the pandemonium of the disciples surrounding him captures the profound synthesis of the painting as a whole: the stillness of Christ and the mathematically ordered space harmonizes and balances with the freedom of movement depicted by the disciples.

What do you notice about Christ's hands? What do you think that means?

Note how his palms are inverse of one another, his left palm is directed upward, while his right palm is directed downward toward the table. As Cynthia Pearl Maus has observed, Christ's hands express his humanity and divinity. "One hand, with palm downward, seems to say, 'If it be possible, let this cup pass from me.' The other, upturned, receptive, suggests the words, 'Not my will, but thine be done.'"[12] Moreover, his hands appear to gesture towards the monastics who would be eating in the refectory, inviting them to commune with him. Indeed, the table and the room depicted by Leonardo appear to be replicas of the tables in the refectory.

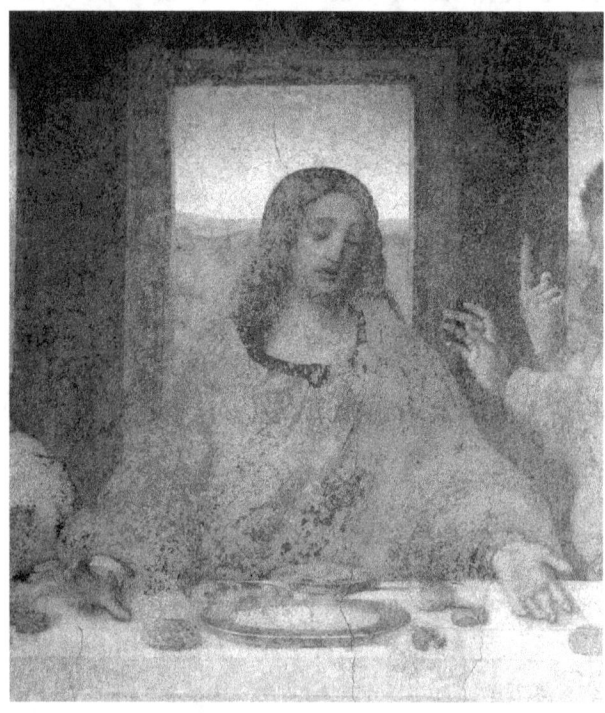

But note what Christ is looking at. His hand, palm upward, lays on the table, a piece of wood. Just next to it is a glass of red wine, signifying blood. Christ is staring at what will happen in mere hours, his giving up his own life for the life of the world. Moreover, the hand opens towards us, inviting us to the hand gestures just above, with James' gesturing towards the window behind Christ, together with Thomas' finger pointing upwards. Note, too, that Thomas, the one who's finger is pointing up, is later– note, after *eight* days (John 20:26) – invited by Christ to probe his wounds with that very finger (John 20:27). We are thus invited

---

[12] Cynthia Pearl Maus, *Christ and the Fine Arts,* (New York: Harper & Brothers, 1959), 291.

to Paradise, which we can access only through the shed blood of Christ as revealed in the bread and wine of the Eucharist, the Tree of Life restored.

CHAPTER 3

Michelangelo, *Pietà* (1498-1500)

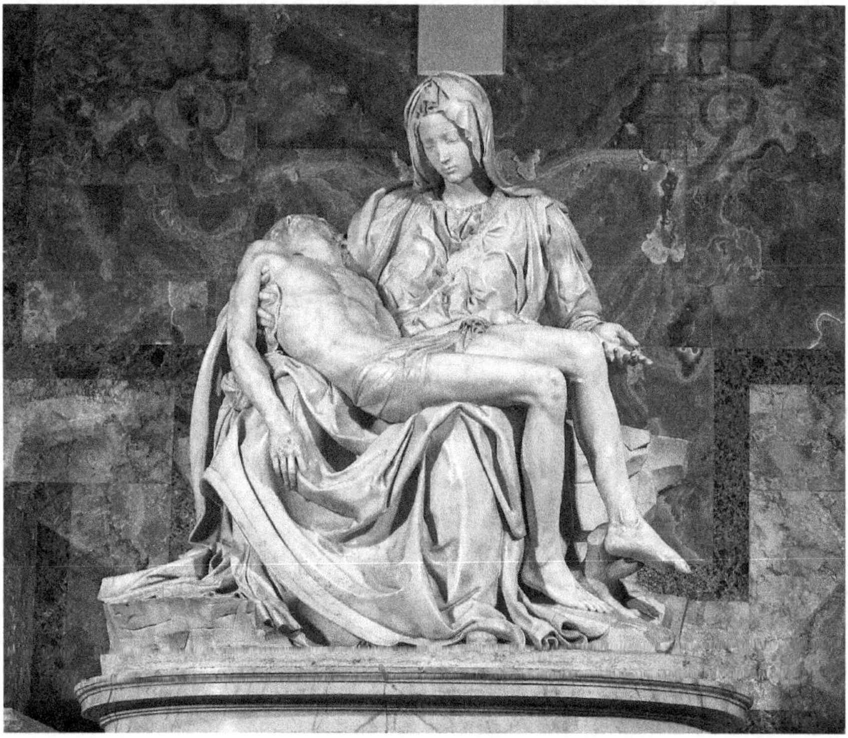

Bio:

Born at Caprese in Tuscany on March 6, 1475, Michelangelo di Lodovico Buonarroti Simoni is considered one of the greatest geniuses of the High Renaissance. Shortly after his birth, his family moved to Florence. His mother died when he was six, and he subsequently went to live with a nanny whose husband was a stonecutter at a local marble quarry. It was here that Michelangelo gained his love for marble. The young artisan became fascinated with the cathedral architecture and frescoes throughout Florence, the epicenter of the Renaissance. At 13, he served as the apprentice to Ghirlandaio, a master fresco painter. He eventually moved to Rome, and what followed was a career that produced some of the greatest artistic monuments in the world, such as the sculpture *David*, the painting of the interior space of the Sistine Chapel in the Vatican, and, of course, the *Pietà*. He died on February 18, 1564, at the age of 88.

Michelangelo was a master of blending together the aesthetic features of the Renaissance: classical notions of beauty with life-like naturalism. For example, Michelangelo was a master of portraying the ancient Greek notion of the heroic body in biblical terms, as evidenced by his *David* sculpture. Far from being a small boy, David is depicted as a muscular male in the heroic nude, something akin to Achilles. With his *Pietà*, he deviated from traditional depictions of Mary by portraying her as extremely young. Many artists followed this example. As an expert of anthropometry, his extremely detailed depictions of the human body contributed to the rise of an art movement known as Mannerism, consisting of elaborate and exaggerated physical proportions and gestures.

The Sculpture:

Michelangelo sculpted the *Pietà* between 1497 and 1500. Traditionally, a *Pietà* is defined as an image of Christ's dead body lying in the arms of his mother Mary.[13] Michelangelo's *Pietà* was commissioned when he was only 24 years old by the French Cardinal Jean de Bilheres, originally as the cardinal's funeral monument. Michelangelo secured a block of Carrara marble, which he claimed to be the most perfect marble block he ever worked with. Out of the block and through Michelangelo's chisel, what scholars have called a 'miracle of marble' emerged. It measures five feet nine inches wide and six feet five inches tall, and is the only work that Michelangelo ever signed, in response to overhearing someone credit the work to another sculptor. He carved his name into Mary's sash: "Michelangelo Buonarroti, Florentine, made this." He later regretted what he did, seeing it as an expression of vanity, and vowed never to sign another work.

Optional Discussion Prompt:

Why do you think Mary is depicted as so much larger than Christ?

Give the students about 10 minutes to write down their observations while gazing at the painting.

Analysis:

What do you notice about the sculpture? What do you find interesting?

The extraordinary detail in the voluminous folds of Mary's garment is simply unprecedented; the flowing drapery of her garments are carved deeply into the marble awakening a

---

[13] Rumy Hilloowala and Jerome Oremland, "The St. Peter's *Pietà*: A Madonna and Child? An Anatomical and Psychological Reevaluation," *Leonardo,* vol. 20, no. 1 (1987): 87-92, 87.

cascade of shadow and complexity; it's frankly, beyond extraordinary. Mary, too, is disproportionately large in relation to the body of Christ. It is often observed that were she to stand, she would tower over Jesus. Mary's head is tilted forward towards Jesus while his head is thrown back, his neck exposed. The face of Mary is unusually young; she in fact appears as a youthful maiden, not the elder mother of a mature man.

What shapes do you see represented in the sculpture, and what do they signify?

It is both triangular and circular. If we see Mary's head as a vertex, we can see a pyramid-like pattern going down towards her shoulders, down to Christ's elbow on one side and her left hand on the other. And yet, her garment around and underneath the body of Christ flows in a circular fashion, with the hem drawing our eyes to Christ's right foot and then his left food slightly elevated, which is complemented by the

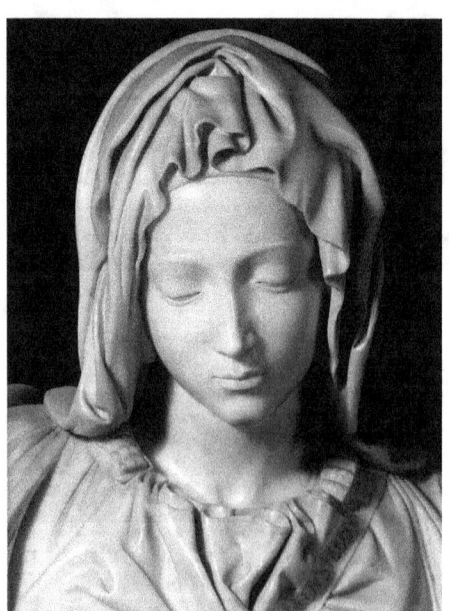

folds of her dress drawing us upward towards Christ's knees, his right leg slightly elevated above his right, and to Mary's left hand, completing the swirling motion.

The triangle represents the Trinity while the circle represents eternity. These two shapes combine to illuminate the unique feature of Mary's youthful countenance. In Dante's

Divine Comedy, with which Michelangelo was intimately familiar, Canto XXXIII begins: "Virgin mother, daughter of your Son, Humbler and higher than all other creatures, Fixed aim and goal of the eternal plan." The extraordinary insight here is that Christ, the eternal Son of God, as a member of the Holy Trinity, is in fact the originator of Mary. This is the mystery that Dante contemplates and seems to find its way embedded in the marble of Michelangelo; being consubstantial with the Father, Jesus is the father of Mary from all eternity. This would explain why Mary appears so young and Jesus appears as a grown, bearded man.

How is Mary holding Jesus, and what is its significance?

She holds up his right arm, so that the weight of his body is drawn into her own, like she's cradling her infant son. He's draped across her lap in congruity with the linen cloth beneath his body as well as her flowing garments. Mary cradles his head like a child's, and his body arched around Mary's is akin to a child being held. Note, too, the fingers of Christ's right hand, how they seem to clasp the dramatic fold of Mary's garment.[14]

This has led to the interpretation that Mary and the viewer are looking at two different visions of Jesus. Mary is actually cradling her child, the baby Jesus, wrapped in a cloth, while we are viewing the baby in terms of his future fate, as the recently crucified Christ. There is thus the convergence of two timelines in the sculpture.

And yet, Mary's face is not without a sense of sorrow or, perhaps better, surrender. This is particularly depicted by her

---

[14] Hilloowala, "St. Peter's *Pietà*," 88-9.

left hand, that appears to be offering her son to the Father in a gesture of prayer. Note, how we're drawn to her left hand: the drape of her garment points upwards towards Christ's knees, the left lifted up slightly above the right, which draws our eyes to Mary's hand, in a posture of prayer, surrendering her son, who is the Son of God, back to God.

Perhaps Mary, too, is seeing the future cross in the face of her little child.

What do you find noticeable and interesting about Christ's body? What is its significance?

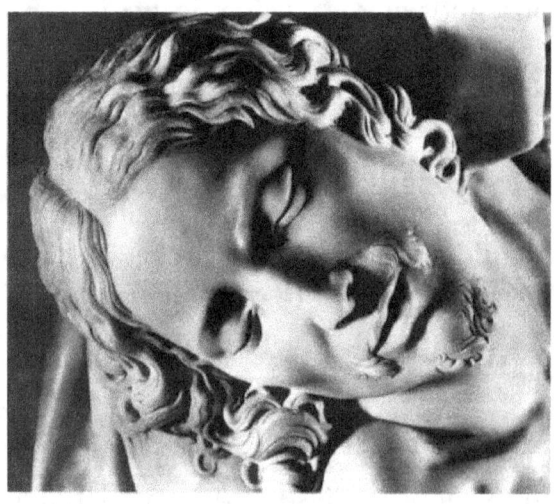

One of the widely recognized characteristics of the Christ figure is the absence of marks from his passion. His body is relatively untouched from any signs of the torture of scourging and, save for the relatively small holes in his hands and feet, crucifixion. Christ's face looks as if he's asleep. He is quiet and peaceful. There are no scars on his head from the crown of thorns. Interestingly, the very slight trace of the lance that speared him is on his left side, almost hidden, rather than on the more traditional right side of his body.

Scholars have noted that the body of Christ appears in some ways to be more alive than dead. When we combine this observation with the youthful appearance of Mary, we begin to see the emergence of eternal life and incorruptible beauty. The combination of her youthful features and Christ's relatively unscathed body signify Christ's victory over sin and death. As such, Christ appears as the New Adam who both receives and takes away the sin and death of the original Eve, to whom was promised a seed who would crush the head of the serpent while his own heel is bruised (Genesis 3:15). The *Pietà* thus depicts Mary, the New Eve, holding the fulfillment of this divine promise in her arms.

CHAPTER 4

Raphael, *School of Athens* (1509-1511)

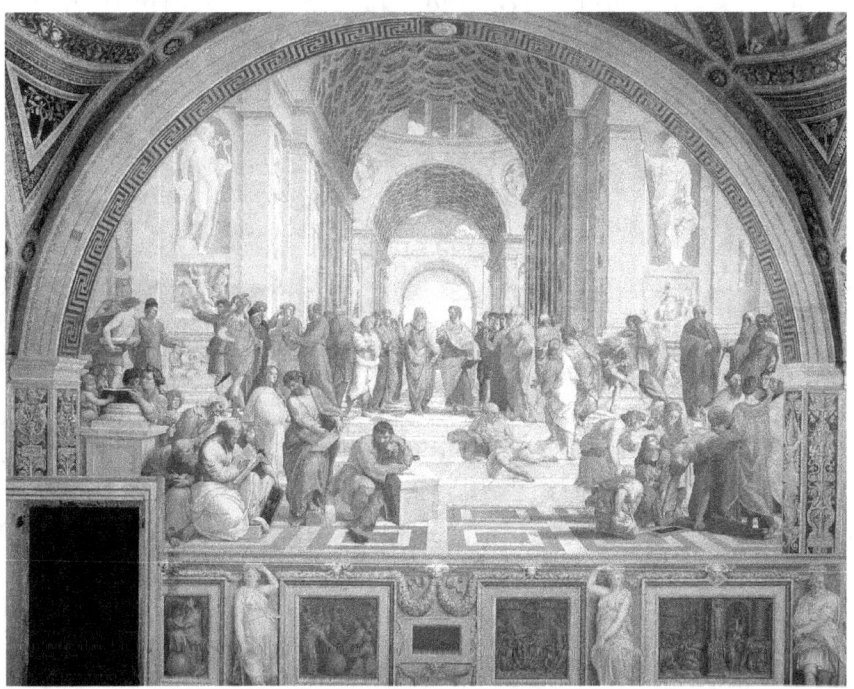

Bio:

Raffaello Sanzio da Urbino was born on April 6, 1483, in Urbino, Italy. He studied painting under Pietro Perugino. His premiere work was the Baronci altarpiece for the church of Saint Nicholas of Tolentino in Città di Castello. In 1508, at the age of 25, Pope Julius II commissioned Raphael to paint frescoes in the library of the Papal Apartments, a room known as the Stanza della Segnatura in the Vatican, and in 1514, the pope appointed him as his chief architect. Raphael is known particularly for a series of Madonnas, portraits of Mary holding the baby Jesus, the final one being his last completed work. He died suddenly on the day of his 37th birthday, April 6, 1520.

Together with Michelangelo and Leonardo da Vinci, Raphael completes what many consider the traditional trinity of the greatest masters of the High Renaissance.

The Painting:

The *School of Athens* began in 1508, when Pope Julius II commissioned the 25-year old Raphael to paint the library of the Papal Apartments, a room known as the *Stanza della Segnatura*. The room was to have four murals painted, one on each side, with each fresco representing one of the four grand topics of knowledge: theology, philosophy, law, and poetry. This painting is of course a grand contemplation of philosophy, specifically, the harmonious synthesis between theology (Christian) and philosophy (Greek), the spiritual and the physical, the heavenly and the worldly.

Optional Discussion Prompt:

How do you see the Seven Liberal Arts (grammar, dialectic, rhetoric, arithmetic, geometry, music, and astronomy) represented in this painting?

Give the students about 10 minutes to write down their observations while gazing at the painting.

Analysis:

Who are the two men at the center? And why is one pointing up and the other down?

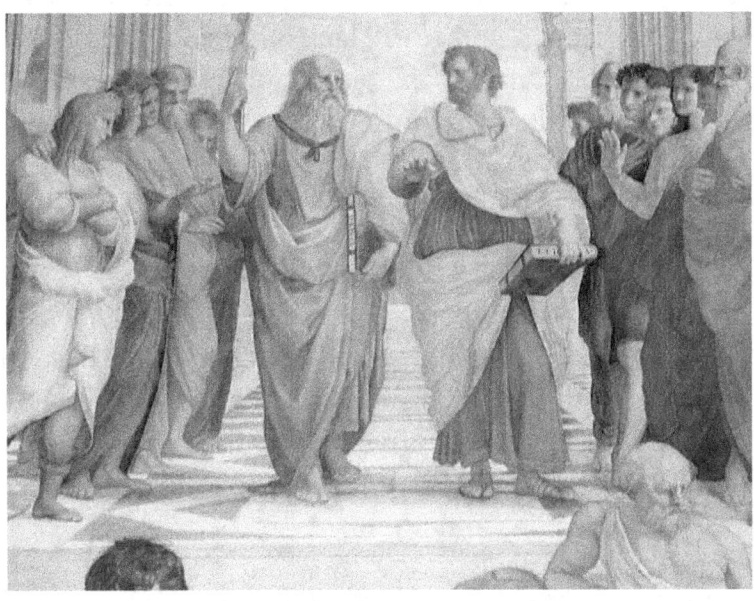

The mural centers on two figures, Plato and Aristotle, the two great philosophers of classical Athens. Plato is pointing upwards to the world of the heavenly ideals or forms (depicted by the blue sky), while Aristotle is gesturing with all five fingers downward, to the world of the senses.

What's significant about the books each one is holding?

Plato holds his work the *Timaeus,* representing his cosmology, while Aristotle holds his work *Ethics,* signifying moral theory. These two works correspond to the two main categories of classical philosophy: *natural* and *moral*. Raphael seems to be drawing from a tradition going back to the 13th century and St Bonaventure which discusses the idea that Plato is about wisdom and Aristotle is about knowledge, the former looking towards upper things, the latter lower things.[15] The *Timaeus* is about the cosmos, whereas Aristotle is holding the *Ethics* which is about life here on earth, as it were.

Interestingly, there is a medallion on the ceiling above the fresco which had an image of lady philosophy holding two books on natural and moral philosophy. The fresco would thus be reflecting the medallion.

What's significant about the vaulted ceiling above them?

Above Plato and Aristotle is a vaulted ceiling that is indicative not of Greek but of Roman architecture, such as the Roman pantheon. Indeed, the ceiling is pillared by two statues, one of Apollo, the Greek god of light, archery, and music, and the other Athena, the goddess of wisdom, in her Roman guise as Minerva. Raphael has thus harmonized together the two great classical cities, Athens and Rome.

Can you guess the identity of some of the philosophers depicted in this painting?

Altogether, there are 58 philosophers depicted in the fresco. Given that Raphael left no identification list, the identity of the philosophers continues to be a point of contention. But there is a consensus regarding the arrangement of the philosophers, as well as some of their identities. Raphael appears to have divided the philosophers into two main groups, the *idealists* to the left and the *realists* to the right, those who focus on the world as a reflection of heavenly perfection vs. those who focus on the world in itself.

---

[15] https://www.bbc.co.uk/programmes/b00j7txt.

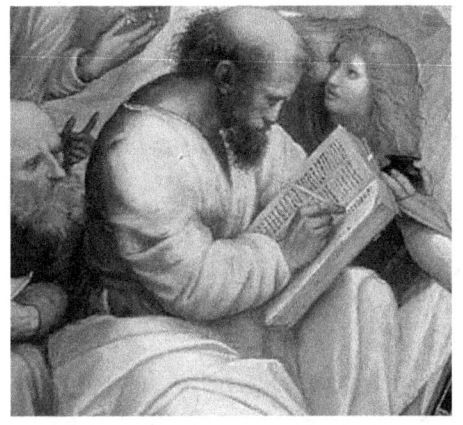
Among the idealists, we see Socrates arguing with his disciples. Another notable is Epicurus, wearing a crown of fig leaves. Next, we can see Pythagoras diagraming what is called the *tetraktys*, 1+2+3+4=10, which is the mathematical key to unlocking the music of the spheres. And we can see Heraclitus, the first philosopher to use the term *Logos* as the organizing principle of the universe, at the bottom, his left elbow on the pedestal propping his head up.

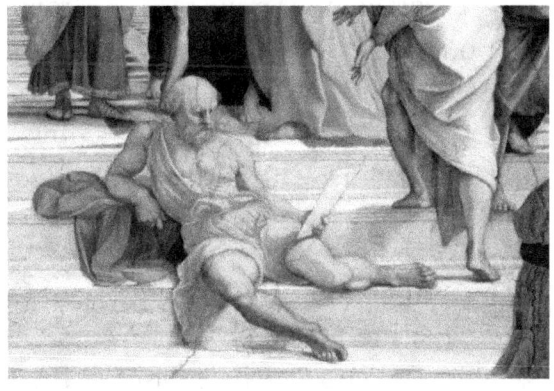
On the realist side, we see Diogenes the cynic sprawled out on the steps; holding the globes of the earth and sky is the astronomer Ptolemy and the geographer Strabo respectively. Then we see Euclid in front of his four students, bent over drawing out a theorem comprised of a six-pointed start with two parallel lines and a diagonal at its center.[16]

---

[16] "Raphael's School of Athens," http://scholarship.claremont.edu/cgi/viewcontent.cgi?article=1050&context=jhm.

But this painting is ultimately about synthesis, how wisdom and knowledge come together in a unified whole. It seems, left to its own, the painting never quite explains how knowledge and wisdom interrelate; after all, the philosophers representing the idealist and realist views are on opposite sides. So how do wisdom and knowledge, the heavenly and the earthly, come together as one?

Notice the colors of Plato's and Aristotle's robes. Plato is donning a red robe over purple clothing, while Aristotle is wearing a blue robe over brown clothing. From the vantage point of the four elements, red and purple are associated with fire and ether/air respectively, while blue and brown correspond to water and earth. But note how Aristotle's blue cloak overlaps Socrates' red cloak. Do you remember the colors that iconography reserves for Christ? A blue robe on the outside and red on the inside! Do you see a correspondence? Raphael has just answered the question of how wisdom and knowledge come together in terms of Colossians 2:3: "in Christ are hidden all the treasures of wisdom and knowledge."

Raphael appears to be drawing here from a distinction made by Augustine between knowledge (*scientia*) with wisdom (*sapientia*). Knowledge involves the temporal world while wisdom involves eternal reality. It is only through *sapientia* that the soul can be directed toward eternal reality and therefore constitute a true image of God. However, the soul is trapped in *scientia*; humanity, plagued by the imprisonment of the Fall, lacks the spiritual resources constitutive of *sapientia*. This anthropological chasm between *scientia* and *sapientia* is bridged by the Incarnation, the Word made flesh, "*in whom are hidden all the treasures of wisdom and knowledge* (Col 2:3)" (*Trinity*, XIII.24). It is thus through faith in Christ, the Incarnate Word who is the Truth, that our souls are graced with *sapientia* and thereby become truly human.

If Plato and Aristotle transform into symbols of the Incarnation, what then becomes of the background immediately behind them, especially as it is outline by the arch?

The blue sky and arch outline transform into a halo.

How does the vaulting ceiling transform?

The vaulted ceiling transforms into a replica of the vaulted ceiling in St. Peter's Basilica in the Vatican.

And notice, further, the layout of the building: what is its form?

The building recedes behind Plato and Aristotle and extends outward on both sides of them, thus making the shape of a cross. Raphael has thereby harmonized the *three* great classical cities: Jerusalem, Athens, and Rome, as all three come together in the transformative death and resurrection of Christ.

CHAPTER 5

Caravaggio, *The Beheading of Saint John the Baptist* (1608)

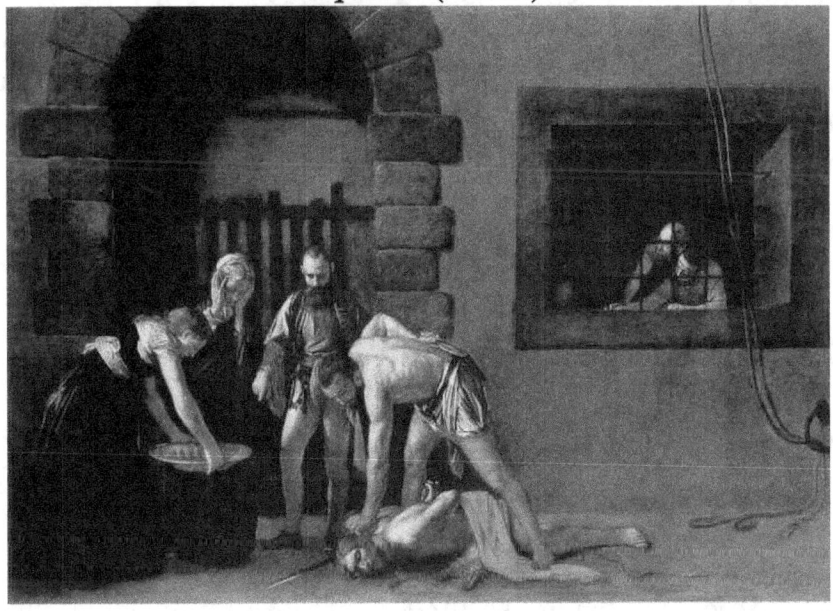

Bio:

Michelangelo Merisi da Caravaggio was born in Milan in 1571. His family relocated to a town called Caravaggio in order to escape a plague that was ravaging Milan; however, both his father and grandfather died shortly after arriving.

Caravaggio's mother died a few years later, and he began an apprenticeship with the painter Simone Peterzano back in Milan. He subsequently moved to Rome where he quickly gained notoriety for his tenebrism, a painting technique that dramatically illuminates its subject matter with stark contrasts between light and darkness. Unfortunately, Caravaggio was prone to brawling and arrests (his police records were voluminous), and in May of 1606, he ended up killing his former friend in what appears to have been a gang fight, resulting perhaps from a quarrel over debt. He fled outside Rome's jurisdiction to Naples, and then eventually to Malta, where he was received by the Knights of the Order of St. John of Jerusalem, Rhodes, and Malta, a chivalric order established in the eleventh century during the Crusades. Caravaggio was actually installed in the order in 1608, but was quickly expelled, most likely the result of another brawl. He moved to Sicily and then back to Naples, where he died shortly thereafter in 1610.

The Painting:

The Beheading of Saint John the Baptist is considered perhaps Caravaggio's greatest work, and a masterpiece among the works of Western painting. It's a very large painting, measuring 12 feet by 17 feet. Caravaggio painted *The Beheading* in his final years of life. Having just killed his former friend in a fight, he fled Rome to the island of Malta in order to escape being executed, which ironically would have been by beheading.[17] Upon his installation into the Knights of the Order of St. John of Jerusalem, Rhodes, and Malta, some

---

[17] Heidi J. Hornik, "Confronting the Powers," https://www.baylor.edu/content/services/document.php/125483.pdf.

believe that *The Beheading* was offered in lieu of a financial donation to the order usually given by those newly installed. It remains the only extant work that Caravaggio signed, interestingly in the blood of St. John the Baptist.

Optional Discussion Prompt:

Who is the real prisoner in this picture?

Give the students about 10 minutes to write down their observations while gazing at the painting.

Analysis:

What do you find interesting about this painting?

Notice the characteristics of the Caravaggio's tenebrism, the dramatic illumination of particular characters in the painting contrasted by dark shadowy backgrounds. There are seven characters that can be seen: two women (one young and the other old), a Jailor, an Executioner, John the Baptist, and two prisoners. The painting is punctuated by vibrant reds, pure whites, and warm yellows.

What do you notice about the Executioner?

There are several things here. The painting draws our eyes to the Executioner; in many respects, he's the center of the painting. He's bent over, his muscular left arm holding the head of John, while his right hand unsheathes the *misericorde,* a long knife that will complete the beheading begun by the sword now discarded by John's head. He is mostly unclothed, donning only a white undergarment, and stands straddled over John, the dirty toes of his left foot situated on the red fabric draped over John's dying body.

What do you notice about John the Baptist?

John is depicted as dying, his eyes half closed, yet his face is marked by a peaceful serenity. His arms are bound behind his back, and his body is partially covered by a red garment. He lies on top of a lamb's fleece. Blood is flowing from his neck onto the floor.

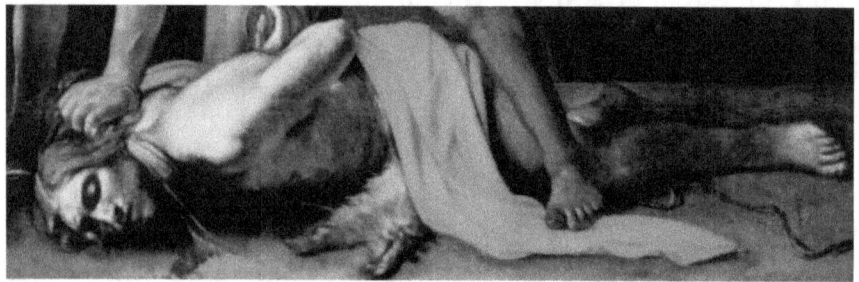

Biographer Helen Langdon says about the Beheading of the Baptist:

> It is an ignoble scene. John does not kneel as is customary in art, but is brought low on the ground, and his body is trussed like that of a sacrificial lamb, his hands tied behind his back, his red cloak suggesting blood, and a rope snaking across the floor. Action is arrested, and the group, earthbound, downward-looking, is utterly still, gesture and expression muted. Caravaggio emphasizes the reality of John's death in a gloomy prison, unattended by angels; the threat of the prison, the terror of torture and punishment, are powerful – this was a place where justice was meted out."[18]

---

[18] Helen Langdon, *Caravaggio: A Life* (London: Pimlico Press, 1998), 357.

What is the significance of the red garment and lamb's fleece?

This is an allusion to Christ, the sacrificial lamb of God who takes away the sins of the world through his own shed blood.

Notice the rope around John's left hand; it forms a perfect circle as it extends through his index finger. What do you think that signifies?

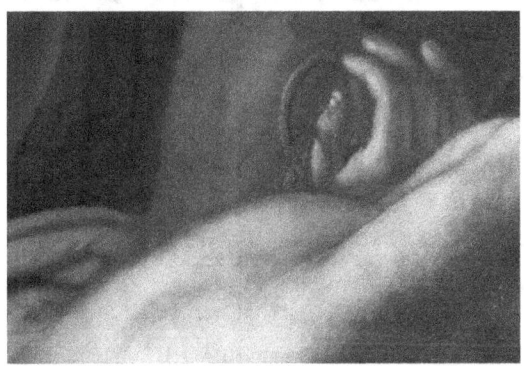

It resembles the shape of a pyx, a small round container used in the Catholic church to store and transport the consecrated Eucharistic host. It is also indicative of the emblem of the Order of St. John whose symbol was a Eucharistic circle.[19] Both serve to corroborate that John is a type of Christ sacrificially offered up to God.

What do you notice about the Executioner's sword on the ground?

The Executioner's sword lies next to John's head. It is both in shadow and light; the darkness depicts the evil nature of his execution, but the light depicts John's identification with Christ, through whom God has redeemed the world.

---

[19] https://yshefer.wordpress.com/2014/09/20/conclusions-regarding-the-painting-by-caravaggio-of-the-beheading-of-john-the-baptist-in-the-co-cathedral-valletta-malta-2/.

How do the postures of John the Baptist and the Executioner relate to one another?

Both John and the Executioner are face down. However, the Executioner's relative nakedness and dirty feet combine with his bent over posture to depict as if he were walking on all fours, perhaps depicting him as an animalistic brute beast. The posture of his right arm and hand complements John's left arm and hand, which is bound. Perhaps Caravaggio is suggesting that the Executioner, too, is bound, in this case, by the fallen nature of the world. The Eucharistic shape of John's tied up hands indicates that he is free, as he is incorporated into the transformative death and resurrection of Christ.

What do you see regarding the two women on the left?

There is a young girl and an old woman. The younger girl appears to be a servant rather than Salome, as some interpret her. The younger girl is focused on the salver on which the head of John the Baptist will be placed. She is in many respects a mirror image of the Executioner; she's bent over, her slender right arm holding the salver complementing the Executioner's muscular left arm holding the head which will be placed on the salver. She is clothed in a white garment that curves around her shoulder and armpit akin to the Executioner's white garment curving around his loins.

The old woman's face is one of grief and pain over the execution, as her detailed hands cover her ears and, in a sense, holding her own head. One commentator argues that the contrast between the young girl and old woman represents the New and Old Testaments, as the "head" of the

Old Testament law is removed from Israel and placed into the salver of the church.[20]

What do you observe regarding the Jailor at the center of the main group?

His posture indicates his authority over the grim scene. He's pointing to the salver as if to instruct where to place the head. Note his jail keys dangling from his waste over his right leg, accentuated by their shadow on his pants. He is a clear symbol of power and authority.

How do the two prisoners watching the scene relate to the painting?

At one level, they can be seen as foreshadows of the two prisoners that would be crucified on either side of Christ. However, notice that they are imprisoned behind bars. Note, too, the gate spanning the aperture behind the execution scene. The prisoners and the gate combine to reveal that even though the Jailor may think he has authority and the keys to freedom, the overall painting reveals that he is actually the prisoner; the fenced-in aperture reveals that the Jailor is in his own prison; his keys mean nothing in a world imprisoned by sin, death, and the devil. It is John the Baptist who is actually free, as he is identified with the redemptive work of Christ who alone conquers the imprisoning elements of this world.

What is the significance of the shadow effect throughout the painting?

---

[20] https://www.buffalo.edu/content/dam/www/nemla/NIS/XXXVIII/NeMLAIS16-8-Giardino.pdf.

It gives the sense that they are in a mass sepulcher or tomb. It depicts the darkness of the souls of those committing this murder, which is reflective of the darkness of the entire world.

CHAPTER 6

Rembrandt, *The Return of the Prodigal Son* (c. 1668)

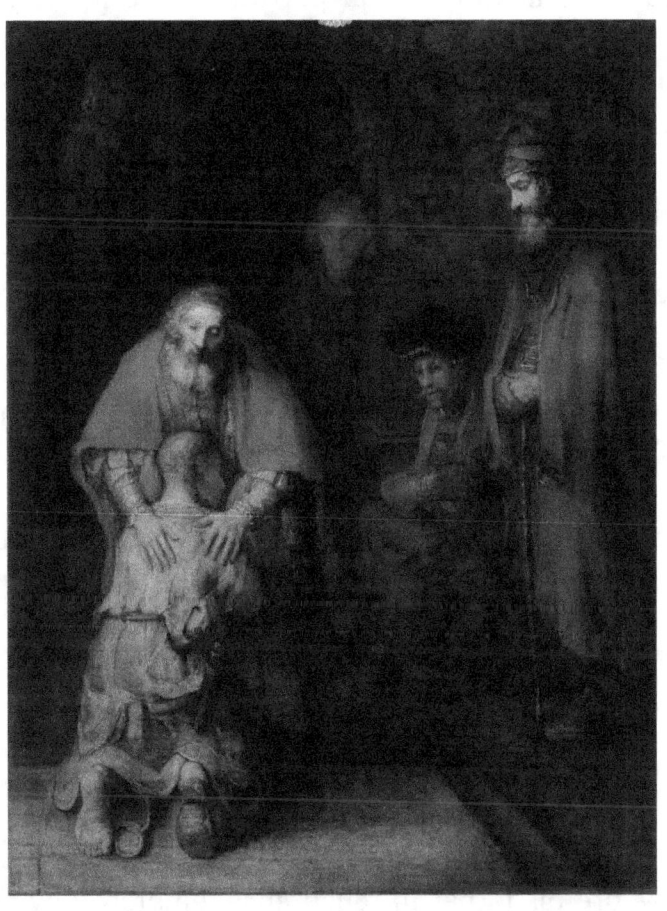

Bio:

Rembrandt Harmenszoon van Rijn was born on July 15, 1606 in Leiden, Netherlands. He was classically educated at the Latin School in Leiden, and subsequently trained under the painters Jacob van Swanenburgh and later by Pieter Lastman. Swanenburgh seems to have influenced Rembrandt's use of light surrounding his painted subjects, while Lastman mentored him in painting biblical and historical scenes. In 1624, Rembrandt opened a studio in Leiden, where he began to receive commissions; and then, in 1631, he moved to Amsterdam as a professional portraitist. He married Saskia van Uylenburgh in 1643, and together they had four children, three of whom died in infancy. Though Rembrandt's career flourished as a painter and a teacher, he seems to have been unable to live within his means and appears repeatedly to have squandered his wealth. He died on October 4, 1669 in Amsterdam, having never left the Dutch Republic in his lifetime.

Rembrandt is considered one of the giants of the Dutch Golden Age, a time of unparalleled artistic, economic, and scientific flourishing in the seventeenth-century. He is indeed counted as one of greatest artists to have ever lived. Perhaps his greatest legacy is his lifetime of paintings that portray the entire life of Christ.

The painting:

The Return of the Prodigal Son is one of Rembrandt's final works, completed around 1668, within a year of his death. It depicts a scene from the Parable of the Prodigal Son as told by Jesus in Luke 15:11-32. Having returned home, the prodigal kneels before his father in repentance, embraced by paternal forgiveness and grace. The elder son stands to the right, while a number of other figures are present but partially hidden by dark shadowing. The painting is considered a masterpiece of Christian art, and possibly Rembrandt's greatest work.

Optional Discussion Prompt:

If you could, how would you paint *forgiveness*?

Give the students about 10 minutes to write down their observations while gazing at the painting.

Analysis:

What do you notice about the painting? What strikes you as interesting?

In one sense, the son is depicted in a manner indicative of what he's become. Remember, he began with the riches of his father's inheritance, and now he's been humbled into a swine herder, he's kneeling on the very ground they crawl on, his hair and clothing are disheveled. We can see the wealth of the father in his glowing red cape and ornate outfit in contrast to the ragged clothing, worn sandals, and scarred feet of the son. The red is a sign of majesty and power. The son responds in humility, asking for forgiveness. The sword at the son's right side is the only token of his past glory.

What do you make of the man standing to the right?

The man standing to the right is younger than the father but older than the son, so we have a clear indication of the older brother. He seems to be standing with disdain while leaning on his stick. He too wears royal clothing.

What's the significance of the father and elder brother, along with all of the other unspecified figures in the painting, standing side by side in the painting?

Rembrandt contrasts the father, who embodies forgiveness, with the elder brother, who embodies a sense of the unforgiveable. The judgment and disdain for the prodigal's sin embodied by the elder brother and other unidentified witnesses reveals that the forgiveness of the father is unconditional. In the words of Constantine V. Proimos:

> What Rembrandt seems to wish to articulate in his picture by siding the father's forgiveness with the older brother's unforgivable attitude, by essentially splitting the patriarchal authority into forgiveness and the unforgivable, is that forgiveness is being granted and ought to be granted without conditions.[21]

In terms of the unspecified figures, Proimos notes that it is part of the pictorial tradition to which Rembrandt belongs to have a number of secondary figures unspecified in the painting.[22]

Why does the painting seem to center on the hands of the father?

In his book, *The Return of the Prodigal Son: A Story of Homecoming,* Henri Nouwen observes that the father's hands are the true center of the painting:

---

[21] Constantine V. Proimos, "Forgiveness and Forgiving in Rembrandt's Return of the Prodigal Son," *Art, Emotion and Value,* 5th *Mediterranean Congress of Aesthetics,* 2011, 297.
[22] Proimos, "Forgiveness," 294.

> On them all light is concentrated; on them the eyes of the bystanders are focused; in them mercy becomes flesh; upon them forgiveness, reconciliation, and healing come together, and, through them, not only the tired son, but also the worn-out father find their rest.[23]

The laying on of hands is very significant in the Bible. In the Book of Acts, hand-laying is one of the primary means of conferring the gift of the Holy Spirit (e.g. Acts 8:14-17). However, in the Jewish patriarchal tradition, it also involves the conferring of blessing upon one's sons, as we see with Jacob's blessing of his sons in Genesis 48:8-22.

The two significances of the single gesture can be seen as converging in the Greco-Roman practice of *manumission*, the act of an owner freeing his slave by laying his hands on him or her and bestowing emancipation. Against the backdrop of the prodigal's willingness to be a slave in his father's house (Luke 15:17-19), the father's gesture reveals his freeing his son from slavery.

Moreover, against the backdrop of Jacob's blessing, he is being reinstated, as it were, into his father's household. And with the laying on of hands in Acts in view, the father is conferring upon his son the gift of the Holy Spirit.

The Return of the Prodigal Son is thus a portrait of us all. We are all welcomed home unconditionally by the Father as we through the Spirit are adopted as sons and heirs of the kingdom (Galatians 4:1-7).

---

[23] Henri J.M. Nouwen, *The Return of the Prodigal Son: A Story of Homecoming* (New York: Doubleday, 1994), 96.

CHAPTER 7

Dante Gabriel Rossetti, *Ecce Ancilla Domini* (1850)

Bio:

Gabriel Charles Dante Rosetti was born on May 12, 1828 in London, England. He was the eldest son of Italian nobleman and scholar Gabriele Pasquale Giuseppe Rosetti who emigrated to England. Though his father was Roman Catholic, Gabriel was baptized into his mother's Anglican faith and educated at King's College School. He liked to place Dante at the beginning of his name for publications in honor of Dante Alighiere, the author of the *Divine Comedy.* After a brief period at the Royal Academy, he studied painting under Ford Madox Brown. He became both a painter and a poet, and in 1848, he founded the Pre-Raphaelite Brotherhood which sought to challenge the artistic conventions of their day. His 1850's paintings almost all used Elizabeth Siddal as his sole model. They were married in 1860, but she committed suicide just two years later after a bout of depression. Rosetti buried a manuscript of his poems in her coffin. He died on April 9, 1882, in Kent, England, and is remembered as one of England's most influential and innovative artists.

The Painting:

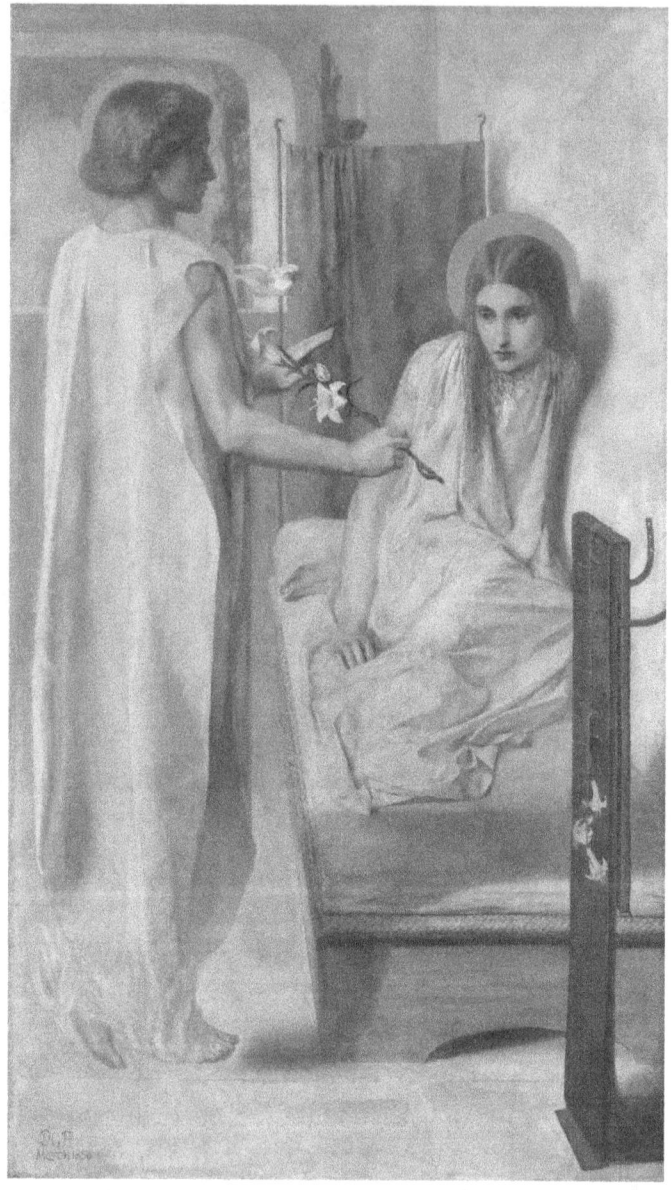

Ecce Ancilla Domini was one of his early paintings, completed in 1850. It is, in many respects, a radical reinterpretation of The Annunciation, the visitation by the angel Gabriel to the Virgin Mary as narrated in the Gospel of Luke. Traditionally, Mary is depicted as standing or sitting on a throne-like chair, her countenance exemplifying a sense of noble contemplation. With Rosetti's painting, Mary is on her bed, drawn back against a wall, and appears rather fearful. Her clothing is radically different as well. Traditionally, Mary's color scheme is the inverse of Christ's: she wears a blue dress wrapped around by a red garment. With Rosetti's rendition, she's completely in white, and the blue and red have been separated, almost bookending her body. The picture is so slender because it was supposed to be part of a diptych, an artwork consisting of two painted panels. The second was never completed.

Optional Discussion Prompt:

Why do you think Mary looks so concerned, or perhaps, even sad?

Give the students about 10 minutes to write down their observations while gazing at the painting.

Analysis:

What are some of the things that you notice in the painting?

There are a number of striking features: the use of white for both Mary and Gabriel, the blue backdrop, and the red loom adorned with lilies complementing the lily held in the hands of Gabriel. Gabriel stands floating above the ground in flames of fire. There's a dove gently flying through the open window.

What is the significance of lilies?

The lily is a symbol of the Virgin Mary. As far back as the Venerable Bede (673-735), theologians have represented Mary with the lily, the white pedals symbolizing her purity. The

Feast of the Annunciation is celebrated on March 25th, at the blossoming of springtime. Indeed, Rosetti has written "March" at the bottom of the canvas, perhaps to commemorate the feast day. The lily is also a symbol of the resurrection, as Easter is marked by floral arrangements of lilies.

What is the significance of white, blue, and red? How does the meaning of the painting become more vivid in light of these colors?

It's important to make sure your students know the meanings behind the classical color schemes: blue signifies eternity, red signifies love, and white represents purity.[24]

Lead the students to explore the meaning of the painting as the colors come together to tell a story. White signifies the purity bestowed by the grace of God. The red loom in the front lower right with white lilies could signify the blood of Christ through which paradise is restored. The second-century text, the *Protoevangelium of James,* narrates how Mary was helping to weave together a new veil for the Jerusalem temple when the Angel Gabriel came to visit her. Her portion of the veil was red, just like the loom in Rosetti's painting.

Note, too, the dove between Gabriel and Mary What is the significance of the dove in Scripture and in this painted scene?

---

[24] Green represents life, yellow and gold signify the presence of God (heaven), black represents death to self, purple represents royalty, brown/bronze represent the earth, silver signifies the sky/clouds.

The dove represents the Holy Spirit (cf. Matthew 3:16). This relationship is accentuated by the blue background of the garment, recalling Christ's baptism, and perhaps even the role of the dove in the Noah narrative. Christ is of course conceived by the Holy Spirit (Luke 1:35).

Let's return to Mary's countenance; why does she appear so concerned?

Invite the students to reflect on this. Finally, show them the shape made by Gabriel's left hand as it intersects with the lily in his other hand: *we see the sign of the cross.* Indeed, Gabriel's two extended fingers signify the two natures of Christ. Mary's eyes are staring at a symbol that is teaching her that not only is she going to give birth to the Messiah, but he will be the sacrificial Lamb of God taking away the sins of the world.

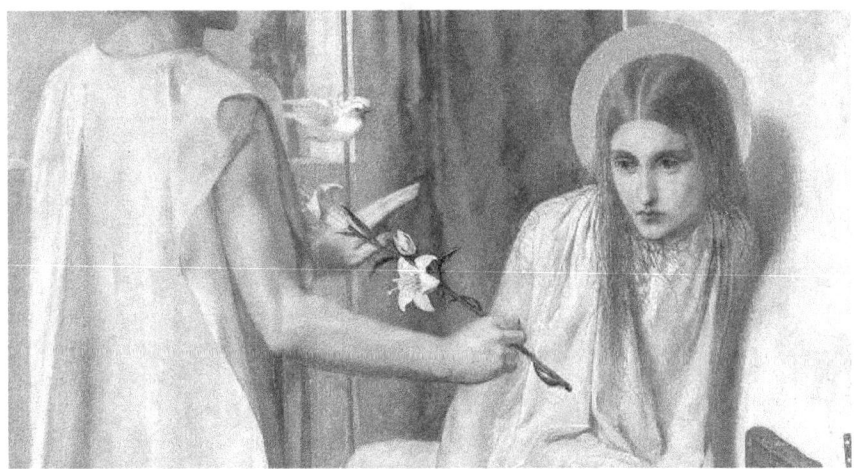

Note, too, that blue and red together make purple, the color of Christ's robe he was forced to wear with his crown of thorns. As comprised of the colors of eternity (blue) and red (love), purple actually declares the gospel of God's eternal love!

But remember, the lily is also a symbol of resurrection. Thus, Mary is staring a profound symbol of the transfiguration of the entire cosmos as it is incorporated into the transformative death and resurrection of Christ.

CHAPTER 8

Vincent van Gogh, *The Starry Night* (1889)

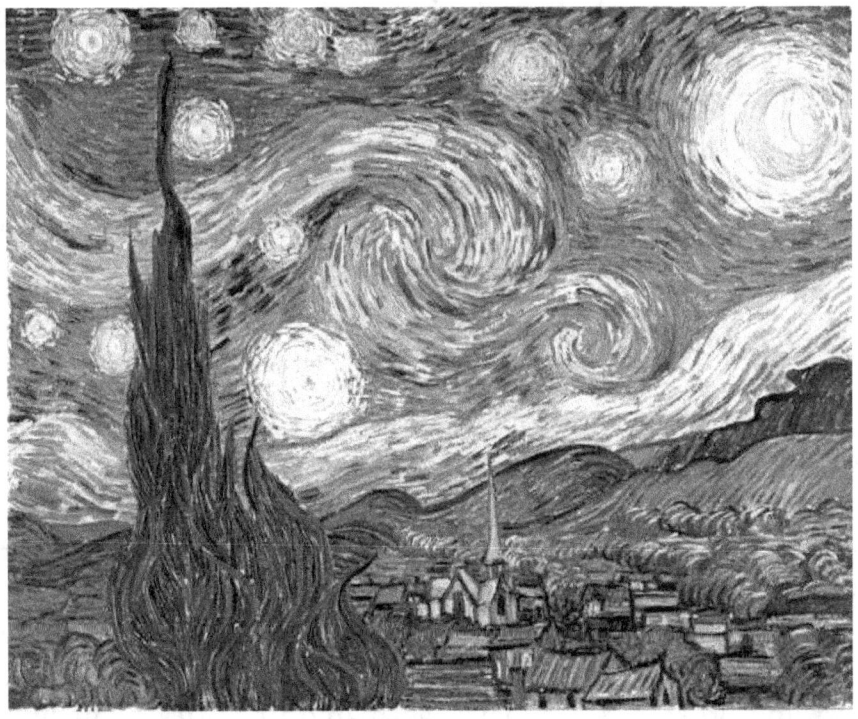

Bio:

Vincent Willem van Gogh was born on March 30, 1853 in Groot-Zundert, Netherlands. His father was a minister in the Dutch Reformed Church. Vincent himself served as a missionary in southern Belgium for a time. His artistic career was largely supported financially by his brother Theo, with whom Vincent kept a sustained correspondence by letter. Van Gogh's artistic output was nothing short of stunning, creating nearly 2,100 artworks in just over a decade. He was one of the great postimpressionist painters, along with Cézanne and Gauguin, all of whom sought to transcend mere physical appearance and reveal the meaning of the world according to their own artistic perceptions.

Van Gogh struggled with mental illness throughout his life, and he is perhaps most (in)famous in popular memory for cutting off his own left ear in a bout of rage, though there are conflicting reports over just how much of the outer ear was removed. Nevertheless, van Gogh did spend time in an out of psychiatric hospitals. Van Gogh died on July 27, 1890, from a self-inflicted gunshot wound. He is remembered as one of the most gifted geniuses of his age.

The Painting:

The Starry Night was painted in June of 1889, towards the end of Van Gogh's life. He was staying in a room at the Saint-Paul asylum in Saint-Rémy-de-Provence, in which he voluntarily entered after severing his left ear. The scene is from the east-facing window of the room. The stunning contrast between the sleepy town and the whirling sky, as well as the deep earthy color contrasts, together with van Gogh's characteristic swirling brush strokes, have led many art critics to include this painting among the greatest works of the nineteenth-century. Since 1941, *The Starry Night* has been part of the permanent collection of the Museum of Modern Art in New York.

Optional Discussion Prompt:

Why do you think van Gogh depicted the sky like a swirling ocean?

Give the students about 10 minutes to write down their observations while gazing at the painting.

Analysis

What strikes you as interesting in this painting?

Note the turbulent swirling brush strokes that turn the sky into ocean-like waves; the concentric circles of white and yellow that surround the stars and the moon. Notice the interesting contrasts throughout the painting, such as the activity in the sky vs. the stillness of the sleepy town, the light of the stars and the darkness of the sky. There is the contrast between the black towering top of the cypress tree to the left against the backdrop of the white church steeple to the right.

What do you find interesting and noticeable about the sky?

It certainly dominates the picture, taking up three-quarters of the painting. The moon and stars fill the sky which swirls around them like the swirling waves of an ocean.

How does the sky contrast with the town below?

The town appears quiet and peaceful, with a number of warm lights shining through their windows, as they surround a central church whose steeple rises into the sky above the backdrop of blue-black mountains.

What do you notice about the cypress tree to the left?

It is very prominent; it almost sticks out of the picture. It stands vertically in stark contrast to the horizontality of the rest of the painting. Its swirling torsion is rather dark and foreboding.

What do cypress trees represent?

In the classical world, the cypress became a symbol of death and mourning. It was used to adorn the statues of Hades/Pluto, the god of the underworld. In Ovid's *Metamorphoses* 10, a young boy named Cyparissus accidently killed his favorite companion, a tamed stag, with his hunting javelin. Because of his incessant mourning, he was turned into a cypress tree, the sap being a perpetual expression of his tears. The endurance of such symbolism can be seen even today, where the cypress remains the principal cemetery tree in Europe.

How many stars are there?

Eleven

Why? Can you think of a biblical story that has eleven stars in it?

In Genesis 37:9, Joseph tells his brothers about his dream of eleven stars, along with the sun and the moon (which seemed to be combined in this painting), all bowing down to him.

Notice how the swirl in the middle of the sky, starting from the far left of the painting, moves in such a way that if you follow it from left to right, it seems to prostrate and bow down.

How would Van Gogh have identified with Joseph?

Joseph was mistreated, thrown into a pit, sold into slavery, and was imprisoned. Van Gogh was dismissed by art critics who simply couldn't recognize his talent, and he eventually found himself in an asylum, from which he painted *Starry Night*.

How does the cypress on the left of the painting fit into this?

Just prior to Joseph's dream of the stars, sun, and moon, he had another dream in Genesis 37:7, where he and his brothers were binding sheaves of wheat, when suddenly his sheaf rose and stood upright while all the others bowed down to it. From this vantage point, perhaps the cypress represents a sheaf of grain standing above all the others.

Given the funerary significance of the cypress, it may also be an acknowledgement by Van Gogh himself that the world would recognize his genius only after his death. This would fit in with Genesis 37 since Joseph was revealing a prophecy that his mistreatment would be reversed, and he would indeed rise up from his imprisonment (like a grave) for the world to revere him.

What would all the lights in the midst of the darkness signify for Van Gogh?

The lights signify hope in the midst of the darkness of his life. "But the sight of the stars always makes me dream," van Gogh once wrote. "Why, I say to myself, should the spots of light in the firmament be less accessible to us than the black spots on the map of France? Just as we take the train to go to Tarascon or Rouen, we take death to go to a star."[25]

As an aside, ask if anyone has seen DreamWork's animated adaptation of the Joseph story, *King of Dreams*. Interestingly, the dream sequences are animated in the style of Van Gogh's *Starry Night*!

---

[25] Vincent van Gogh, Letter to Theo van Gogh, Arles, Monday, 9 or Tuesday, 10 July 1888, http://vangoghletters.org/vg/letters/let638/letter.html.

Thank you so much for purchasing this book!

I hope this book inspired you to gaze all the more deeply into the wonders of art.

If you enjoyed this book, then I'd like to ask you for a favor: Would you be kind enough to leave a review for this book on Amazon? I would so greatly appreciate it!

Thank you so much, and may God richly bless you!

Steve Turley

www.turleytalks.com

Check Out My Other Books

Below you'll find some of my other popular books that are popular on Amazon. Simply go to the links below to check them out. Alternatively, you can visit my author page on Amazon to see my other works.

- *Classical vs. Modern Education: A Vision from C.S. Lewis* http://amzn.to/2opDZju

   Beauty Matters: Creating a High Aesthetic in School Culture https://amzn.to/2L8Ejd7

- *Ever After: How to Overcome Cynical Students with the Role of Wonder in Education* http://amzn.to/2jbJI78

- *Movies and the Moral Imagination: Finding Paradise in Films* http://amzn.to/2zjghJj

- *Health Care Sharing Ministries: How Christians are Revolutionizing Medical Cost and Care* http://amzn.to/2B2Q8B2

- *The Face of Infinite of Love: Athanasius on the Incarnation* http://amzn.to/2oxULNM

- *President Trump and Our Post-Secular Future: How the 2016 Election Signals the Dawning of a Conservative Nationalist Age* http://amzn.to/2B87Q22

- *Stressed Out: Learn How an Ancient Christian Practice Can Relieve Stress and Overcome Anxiety* http://amzn.to/2kFzcpc

- *Wise Choice: Six Steps to Godly Decision Making* http://amzn.to/2qy3C2Z

- *Awakening Wonder: A Classical Guide to Truth, Goodness, and Beauty* http://amzn.to/2ziKR5H

- *Worldview Guide for* A Christmas Carol http://amzn.to/2BCcKHO

- *The Ritualized Revelation of the Messianic Age: Washings and Meals in Galatians and 1 Corinthians* http://amzn.to/2B0mGvf

If the links do not work, for whatever reason, you can simply search for these titles on the Amazon website to find them.

About www.TurleyTalks.com

Are we seeing the revitalization of Christian civilization?

For decades, the world has been dominated by a process known as globalization, an economic and political system that hollows out and erodes a culture's traditions, customs, and religions, all the while conditioning populations to rely on the expertise of a tiny class of technocrats for every aspect of their social and economic lives.

Until now.

All over the world, there's been a massive blowback against the anti-cultural processes of globalization and its secular aristocracy. From Russia to Europe and now in the U.S., citizens are rising up and reasserting their religion, culture, and nation as mechanisms of resistance against the dehumanizing tendencies of secularism and globalism.

And it's just the beginning.

The secular world is at its brink, and a new traditionalist age is rising.

Join me each week as we examine these worldwide trends, discover answers to today's toughest challenges, and together learn to live in the present in light of even better things to come.

So hop on over to www.TurleyTalks.com and have a look around. Make sure to sign-up for our weekly Email Newsletter where you'll get lots of free giveaways, private Q&As, and tons of great content. Check out our YouTube channel (www.youtube.com/c/DrSteveTurley) where you'll understand current events in light of conservative trends to help you flourish in your personal and professional life. And of course, 'Like' us on Facebook and follow us on Twitter.

Thank you so much for your support and for your part in this cultural renewal.

About the Author

Steve Turley (PhD, Durham University) is an internationally recognized scholar, speaker, and classical guitarist. He is the author of over a dozen books, including *Awakening Wonder: A Classical Guide to Truth, Goodness, and Beauty* (Classical Academic Press) and *The Ritualized Revelation of the Messianic Age: Washings and Meals in Galatians and 1 Corinthians* (T&T Clark). Steve broadcasts on current events and cultural trends at TurleyTalks.com. He is a faculty member at Tall Oaks Classical School in Bear, DE, where he teaches Theology and Rhetoric, and Professor of Fine Arts at Eastern University. Steve lectures at universities, conferences, and churches throughout the U.S. and abroad. His research and writings have appeared in such journals as *Christianity and Literature, Calvin Theological Journal, First Things, Touchstone*, and *The Chesterton Review*. He and his wife, Akiko, have four children and live in Newark, DE, where they together enjoy fishing, gardening, and watching *Duck Dynasty* marathons.

www.ingramcontent.com/pod-product-compliance
Lightning Source LLC
Chambersburg PA
CBHW052337220526
45472CB00001B/471